File Management Made Easy

Windows Operating System

NICOLE F. CANNON

WESTBOW
PRESS®
A DIVISION OF THOMAS NELSON
& ZONDERVAN

WestBow Press books may be ordered through booksellers or by contacting:

WestBow Press
A Division of Thomas Nelson & Zondervan
1663 Liberty Drive
Bloomington, IN 47403
www.westbowpress.com
1 (866) 928-1240

ISBN: 978-1-9736-7927-1 (sc)
ISBN: 978-1-9736-7926-4 (e)

Library of Congress Control Number: 2019917989

Print information available on the last page.

WestBow Press rev. date: 02/22/2020

I would like to thank God for His endless encouragement and prodding me to write the book. I also want to thank John and Umckia, for editing, Art for his anecdotes, Catherines' attention to detail and Maman, who is now deceased, and encouraged me to write it. Thank you to all, you know who you are and have not mentioned your names. Thank You!

CONTENTS

INTRODUCTION

The reason for writing this book was my students. They were frustrated with the complexity of the language in a textbook written for beginners. The way I taught the class was to break down the information in the text and have them complete hands-on exercises. One day, several of my students told me, "Ms. Cannon, why don't you write a book about computers, specifically, file management?" I thought about it, and then I wrote this book.

I wrote it so that you will find it easy to understand and be able to easily organize your computer files. Just remember that it takes time and effort on your part. Osmosis does not work here, but diligence and perseverance will get you where you want to go. File management is not difficult, and a little planning (that is not a bad word) will go a long way.

Give it a try, but before you start, always make sure that you pray first and ask the Lord to help you. God is in the computer field also. He understands it better than you think he does. I will tell you a little story.

I had just returned from lunch, and one of the managers had a meeting at 1:00 p.m. He asked me whether the document was ready for the meeting. With confidence, I replied it was. He stood next to me as I logged onto the computer and tried to open up the document. I could not get it to open. I rebooted the system, and still nothing. The manager and I looked at each other, and I did it again. Still nothing. Then a young engineer from the managers group came over and asked what was going on. We told him, and his response was, "Oh, it is probably some gremlin in the system," and he walked away. Now the computer was shut down.

I looked at the manager and spoke with my hands on the computer. "In the name of Jesus Christ, I bind you, Satan. Get off this computer." With the manager still standing there, I rebooted the system, and it came on. I looked at the manager, and he looked at me. We said nothing. I then was able to pull up the document and print it for him in time for the meeting. He was very grateful and in awe of what had just happened, and so was I. You know, there is nothing impossible for God to do. Simply trust Him, His Word, and the Holy Spirit. He said, "Call unto Me, and I will show you great and mighty things," and boy, He sure did. Now, you may laugh, but it is a true story.

It is important not to give up. Call on the Lord, and He will help and teach you by opening your understanding and downloading the information you need to succeed.

Remember one thing: He is on your side. You must do your part, pray, study, read, and do the work. When a difficult situation arises, call, and He will help you.

CHAPTER 1
What Is a Computer System?

This is a basic instruction manual about file management, but before we start there, we need to understand the following.

1. What is a computer system?
2. What are the parts that make up a computer?
3. What is an operating system?
4. What is a central processing unit (CPU)?

What Is a Computer System?

Today, everywhere you go, almost every office has a computer on a desk. Yes, I said almost. When looking for an apartment, I visited a large apartment complex, and they used an electric typewriter to prepare their monthly rent statements. That lady must have been typing for days.

Back to the computer. A computer is an electronic device you use to input information and instructions. The device uses the information according to the instructions you give it. The information is then displayed on a screen (known as the monitor) and stores your information for you to access later, on a hard disk known as the C drive (on your computer there maybe another letter for the hard disk). Computers, or PCs, come in various forms. Look at the list below.

1. All-in-one computers[1] (image is below) are desktop computers where the motherboard and CPU are part of the monitor.

---

[1] http://www.microsoftstore.com/store/msusa/en_US.

An all-in-one computer.

2. Laptops[2] (also known as notebooks) are lightweight and portable.

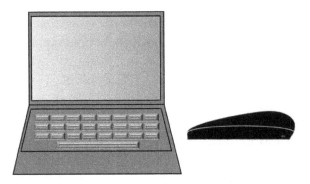

A laptop.

3. Netbooks are small laptops. They can be less powerful, but they have a longer battery life.
4. Tablets are a type of PC and are light and portable.
5. Mobile devices, such as smartphones and tablets are small computers. They have limited battery life, and capabilities compared to a PC.

---

[2] http://www.microsoftstore.com/store/msusa/en_US.

Nicole F. Cannon

The diagram below is an example of a desktop, which was designed to sit on a desk. This model is used to explain the parts that make up a computer.[3]

A desktop computer.

1. Monitor—output device, showing the results of the data you keyed into the computer.
2. Modem—a device enabling computers to transmit data over telephone or cable lines.
3. System tower—contains the motherboard, CPU, hard disk, and cards that expand the capabilities of the motherboard. It can be placed on the floor.
4. Mouse—an input device that allows you to issue commands, such as drag, drop, or move text within the document, and scroll from one page to another.
5. Speakers—an audio output device.
6. Printer—an output device that prints the data.
7. Keyboard—a device used to input data into the computer.

---

[3] http://www.microsoftstore.com/store/msusa/en_US.

CHAPTER 2
What Is an Operating System?

"Without an operating system, a computer is a worthless paperweight."[4] You are probably thinking, "Why discuss the operating system? This is supposed to be about file management." Stay with me as I explain. The operating system (OS) is software that manages and coordinates activities on the computer. The OS helps the computer perform essential tasks such as displaying information on the screen and saving data on disks. It contains your file management system, which is accessed by clicking or touching the Windows Explorer icon located on the Windows task bar at the bottom of the screen. See figure 1 below.

Figure 1
Windows Explorer Icon

Image of a file icon for File Explorer. [5]

Recent Windows operating systems were Windows XP, Windows Vista, Windows 7, and Windows 8.1. Now there is Windows 10.[6]

Windows is the name of the operating system, and 8.1 is the version. The previous version was Microsoft Windows 7. The difference between the two is that Windows 7 had a few gestures for the touchscreen, and Windows 8.1 was designed for touchscreen devices such as laptops, tablets, and desktops with a display that is touch activated and runs on computers with a trackpad or mouse.

---

[4] Art Jernberg, IT specialist.
[5] This image was purchased from: http://www.dreamstime.com/stock-photography-laptop-folder-d-screen-image39025532
[6] All references to Microsoft Windows Explorer or Explorer, Vista, XP, Windows 7, 8, or 10 are copyrights of the Microsoft Corporation.

The instructions for file management are similar in Windows 10. The File Explorer folder is located within the task bar located at the bottom of the screen.

The Role of the Operating System

1. Manages the processor
2. Manages random access memory (RAM), a temporary memory
3. Manages input/output (I/O)
4. Manages authorizations
5. Manages file management
6. Manages information
7. Manages execution of applications
8. Access documents, settings, and other resources
9. Selects objects and commands
10. Displays content out of view (vertical scrolling)
11. Stores files
1. Enters and accesses text files

What Makes the Operating System Run? The Software.

Loaded on the computers are two types of software.

a. System software runs the computer and the operating system.
b. Application software, abbreviated as app, is the other software you use to perform tasks such as writing documents, watching a movie, or accessing the Internet.

Let's look at the Windows 8.1 operating system, because it was the software that incorporated touch gestures. If you have a screen with touch capability, you used your fingertips to select data and move it around. Windows 8.1 (as well as XP, Vista, Windows 7, and Windows 10) has the ability to access the Screen Tip by resting your pointer over an icon on the ribbon. It identifies the name of the icon and its purpose in the application. See figure 2 below.

Figure 2

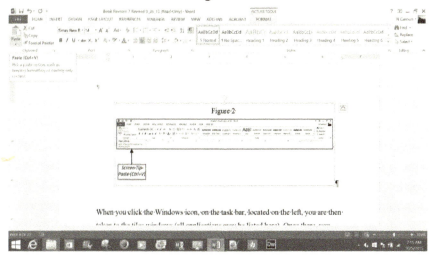

Image of a Screen tip.

We are still working with Windows 8.1. When you click the Windows icon on the task bar, located on the left, you are then taken to the tiles windows (all applications may be listed here). Once there, you will see a down arrow on the bottom left, within a circle. Click on the arrow, and the applications are displayed. To return to your document, click on the arrow, which is now pointing up, move your mouse pointer down to the left, the Windows icon reappears. Click it, and you are back to your document.

Windows 8.1 has a Charms bar, a vertical bar located on the right side of your screen that is accessible at all times. To access the Charms bar, swipe your fingers or move the mouse to the bottom right of the screen. The Charms bar appears on the right, containing the Search, Share, Start, Devices, and Settings icons. These icons allow for quick access to these actions. The Charms bar can be accessed anytime no matter where you are on the screen or what application you are in. You can also press the Windows logo key and the letter C on your keyboard to access the Charms bar. See figure 3 below.

Figure 3

Image of Charms bar from Windows 8.1.

1. "Touch Gestures" allow you to move an object by pressing your finger on the screen and dragging.
2. The Start screen is scrollable by swiping from the right edge of the screen to the left.
3. To select an object or perform an action such as starting an app, tap the object once.
4. Zooming is performed by pinching two fingers to zoom out; move the fingers apart to zoom in.

In the above interactions, you may use a mouse instead of your fingers if you prefer.

Remember the above information refers to Windows 8.1. If you have versions prior to Windows 8.1, or the new Windows 10, you can access your file management system by clicking on the Windows, File Explorer folder icon located on the taskbar, as shown in figure 1 on page 5.

CHAPTER 3
What Is a Central Processing Unit (CPU)?

There are two more important elements we have to talk about, and they are the central processing unit (CPU) and BIOS. Without these, your computer will not boot up.

1. The central processing unit, commonly known as the CPU or the processor, is a silicon chip within a microprocessor, located on the motherboard. The CPU is the brain of the computer, and much of the calculations take place here. In regard to computing power, the CPU is the most important element of a computer system.[7]

2. (bī´ōs) **BIOS** is an acronym for *basic input/output system*, the built-in software that determines what a computer can do without accessing programs from a disk. The BIOS is an important part of any computer system. On personal computers (PCs), for example, the BIOS contains all the code required to control the keyboard, display screen, disk drives, serial communications, and a number of miscellaneous functions.[8]

Remember, without the CPU and BIOS, your computer will not start.

---

[7] https://www.webopedia.com/TERM/C/CPU.html
[8] https://www.webopedia.com/TERM/B/BIOS.html

CHAPTER 4
Vision

Before we begin with file management, it is important that you understand you must have a vision and be organized. Let's begin with vision. In other words, where do you want to go? If you do not have a vision and write it down, then you are not going to get wherever you want to go. So what is your vision, your purpose? What is it that you want to accomplish? If you are not able to answer these questions, you need to stop and do so now. Many of you may be familiar with the word *vision*, but you may not fully comprehend its meaning and importance. Below are two quotes from the same book and verse, but different translations.

> Where there is no vision, the people perish: but he that keepeth the law, happy is he. (Proverbs 29:18 KJV)

> Where there is no revelation, people cast off restraint; but blessed is the one who heeds wisdom's instruction. (Proverbs 29:18 NIV)

What does vision mean?

VI·SION : The ability to think about or plan the future with imagination or wisdom. *'the organization had lost its vision and direction'*[9]

We are going to be speaking from the fifth definition, where you get a revelation from God. If you do not know what you want to do (vision), you will have difficulty achieving your goal. You have to know what it is you are passionate about. Many times your mom and dad know, but you still need to ask God and get his okay. He will answer you. Once you receive that revelation, now you can begin to take the necessary steps to accomplish that goal. Ask the Lord what field you should go into and what

---

[9] https://www.lexico.com/en/definition/vision

college or university you should attend. He knows which one is perfect for you. He helped me with my choice. My experiences and studies were wonderful, and I learned so much. Once you know the field you are going into and the educational institution you will be attending, set a goal that will get you there. Begin by studying the subject. Go to school, get a copy of the catalog, and read what classes you will need to take. Once you do that, apply to the school, make sure it has a good curriculum for your field of study, go to the admissions office, and speak to an academic counselor. You will be on the road to seeing your dreams and vision become a reality. I am not going to tell you it won't take work, because it will. Remember that if you believe in God and in yourself, all things are possible through Christ, who strengthens you, but you will have to persevere.

Do not think that God does not understand computers, or programming for that matter. After all, He is the one who gave humans the idea or vision in the first place, whether or not they acknowledge it. Remember that God is in the midst of computer information systems, programming, engineering, medicine, science, law, and more. When you invite Him in, you will receive wisdom and insight that others will not have. Take a moment now and ask the Lord, "What should I do, and what do I need to do to get there?" Be patient and keep asking, and while you are doing that, begin to read about the area in which you are interested. If you do not have a vision or know where you are going, you will be wandering along a road and making wrong turns and bad choices that will not lead you to your final destination without getting frustrated or stressed, or even perishing along the way, perhaps not achieving your goal.

Now that you have taken a moment to pray, let us go on to the matter at hand. In the next chapter, we are going to discuss organization.

CHAPTER 5

Organization

Without organization, you cannot achieve a well-laid-out plan and reach your goal.

Now, let's look at organization. The meaning of organization, is simply: To put in order: *To arrange files alphabetically or by date.*[10] In other words, *arranging data files, to quickly retrieve them.*[11]

Organization is a word that can cause dread or panic in a lot of people. Are you one of them? Is it something difficult for you to do? Does your computer screen look like the catch-all room at home? That is to say, there are so many files on your screen that it makes you dizzy? Then you say to yourself once again, "I am going to organize these files one day, because this is a ridiculous mess!" Well, that someday has arrived. The time is now.

Whenever something is in disarray, many times we have to look within ourselves. I know I do. When I fret, worry, or get stressed out, I know that I am out of control. Sometimes we cannot do this alone. What you need to do is stop, forget about being embarrassed, and get some help. There are many sources out there where you can get help. You can watch a do-it-yourself television show on how to get organized. You can go to a website such as http://www.organizedtimes.com and http://www.wikihow.com/Be-Organized, and there are many more. You may need someone to walk alongside you and help you with this process. That's okay! Do you know what I do when I have my moments of disorganization? I stop and think to myself, *What is going on here?* Then I will go to my room, pull out my favorite Bible verse, read it, and meditate on it. I allow the Word to get down into my spirit and rejuvenate me. This brings me back to ground zero, that neutral zone where I can think. Your mind has to be clutter

---

[10] Emphasis added by author.
[11] Emphasis added by author.

free. If you need to pray, then pray. It works for me. Once you have a clear mind, do the following.

1. Set aside an amount of time you can complete this task. It may take one hour, two hours, or two days. Whatever it is, just do it!
2. If you are working, you may do it on your lunch hour. If you're at home, pick a quiet time when the kids are napping or in school. If you're single, you must set aside time that works for you. Being busy does not always mean you are progressing and going forward. It may be a subjective move on your part to postpone the inevitable: organization.
3. Get several sheets of paper and a pencil.
4. Label the top of the first sheet "Filenames."
5. Now write down—yes, write down—all the filenames listed on your computer screen. This helps you identify the current files from the old and obsolete files.
6. Get another sheet of paper and label it "Folders."
7. Look back at the Filename sheet, create a name for your first folder, and then list all the files that belong in that folder beneath the name of this first folder.
8. Remember that as you go through and list the file names under the respective folder, cross that file name off your list. This gives you a visual image of how you are doing, and it is nice to see the file names being crossed off as you continue to make phenomenal progress.
9. Keep going, and complete the task.
10. Go over the list and make sure the files are associated with the correct folder.
11. You can take a break for a few minutes. Then return to your computer, create the new folders, and place the assigned files into them.
12. As you do this, you will begin to see more of your computer's desktop and less clutter.
13. If you have two hard drives as I do, one can be designated for work, school and the other for personal documents such as legal documents, taxes and bill payment. If you move your files around,

make sure you make note of that within the file structure by creating a hyperlink to the folder you that contains the data you are looking for.

If you feel stress, that is because you are not able to walk in and quickly get what you need or will need in a few days. When you go to your computer and need to find an old tax file because you are being audited, God forbid you cannot find it. Then what happens? You panic! You get stressed, all the wrong chemicals are released into your system, you are not able to think straight, and you are ready to blame everyone in the family, including the dog or cat. If you are a student and have gathered the research data you needed for your final project, and the due date is in a few weeks, you may hyperventilate if you cannot find the data you needed for your final project. Well, I have some good news: being organized is going to make you one happy camper. Do you want harmony? Then organize your files.

Let's look at the word *organization* and what it means.

The plan is to find your files quickly, and organizing them is the tool to get you there.

Perhaps you are saying, "How can I begin organizing my files? I have other areas that I am having this issue with." I am glad you asked. You have to begin by admitting that you are disorganized and need some help. After all, that is what we are here for: to help each other reach our maximum potential. Now, back to the meaning of organization.

Organization is an act or process to form tools of action, an act of forming or arranging the parts of a compound or complex body so that it can be used for service, and distributing data or objects into "suitable divisions" and being able to properly control or manage the parts to form a unit.

We are interested in arranging parts into suitable divisions so that we can properly control or manage our files to form a well-organized file management system. In other words, we want to have unity and not disharmony of our information. Let's look at an example. Take a drawer full of socks that are loose. What do you do? You take one and try to find the matching pair and color. Now, let's say you open another drawer, and all the socks are organized according to color and style. What is the difference? You can quickly select the socks and get dressed. You are a mighty person who is organized. The same can be so with your data and files.

You must understand that organization is not a bad word, and it doesn't take too long to complete. If you do it from the beginning, it will go quicker than if you have to reorganize. Grab a sheet of paper and a pencil and write out or draw how you want to structure the files. Remember that the plan is to organize your files to find them quicker.

CHAPTER 6
File Management
Structure

A laptop with folders protruding from screen.

Do you have a cluttered desktop, C drive, or USB/thumb drive? Is searching for your files like trying to find a needle in the haystack? Do you have duplicates, and you do not know which one is the most current? Do you have outdated files, and you do not know what to do with them? Well, there is a solution for you, and it is the simple task of file management. The key to managing your files is in understanding Windows Explorer. Windows Explorer gives you a visual perspective of where your files are located. Let's begin to look at this in-depth.

Windows Explorer provides libraries where you can store your files according to the file type. By this I mean pictures will be saved in the Pictures folder, music will go to the Music folder, videos go to the Video folder, and documents are saved in the Documents folder.

Files and Folders

Have you ever seen a list of files on a computer saved from different applications (such as Word, Excel, Access, PowerPoint, Peachtree, and Dreamweaver), and they are listed in one long column in random order? I have, and that is one scary file organization. Yes, you can use the Search button, but just think how easy it would be if your files were organized from the start. Sometimes users do not remember where the files were stored. Well, let's see if I can help.

Organizing Your Files and Folders

Everyone wants to be more productive and efficient. You want to save the files and be able to open them again to make necessary changes, print, or review the data. When you save a file, you should store it within a folder. This folder should be labeled properly for quick access and then stored on a disk.

The computer has a disk known as a hard drive, which stores your folders that contain files for your classes or your job. The key here is to have the ability to quickly retrieve the files.

Desktops, laptops, tablets, and smartphones have a file management system that enables you to store files on a USB drive (flash drives), the C drive, CDs, DVDs, or on the cloud. If you are using and storing many images such as photography or videos or both, make sure your storage device is large enough to hold the data. Images and videos take up a lot of room on a disk, and I recommend that you store them on an external hard drive or, if you wish, on the cloud. This is also known as backing up your data, and it is very important that you do this. If you don't, and your computer crashes, you will regret it.

How to Organize Files and Folders

The first thing you need to understand is that Windows has a hierarchical file system. The files necessary to start your computer are located on level 2. (See figure 4 on the next page.)

Figure 4

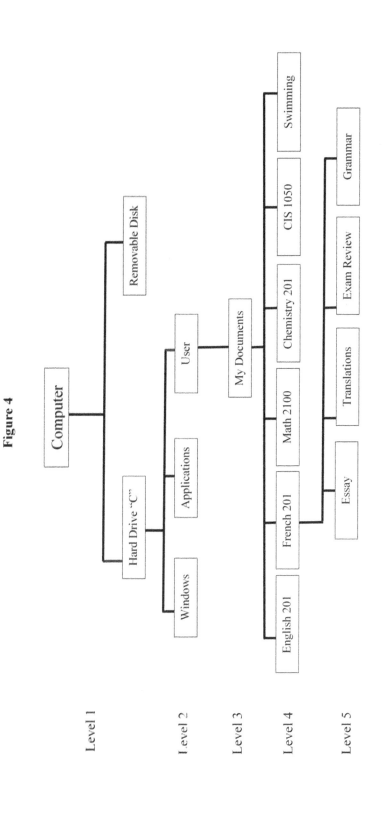

Level 1

Level 2

Level 3

Level 4

Level 5

Level one is known as the root directory, which is the top level of the management file system and contains the system files. The root directory is the top level of the filing system. It is located on the C drive or hard disk of your computer and stores the system files and folders. Do not delete or move these files because your operating system will expect to find them in a certain place. Do not store your files here, because it could interfere with the operation of Windows or an application. Remember—*do not touch,* or else it could cost plenty of dollars to replace them.

On level two of the hierarchy, you will find the software for Windows, applications, and folders for your user accounts, which contain the following.

1. System settings
2. Preferences
3. Other user account information

On level three of the hierarchy, the My Documents subfolder is found. It holds your personal files.

Level 4 of the hierarchy is where you will store your personal files into folders assigned for each class or activity.

On level 5 of the hierarchy are the files stored for, say, your French course.

When you have a folder that has another folder within it, that second folder is known as a subfolder.

CHAPTER 7
Creating a File Management System

How to Create File Folders

Let's begin with an example of how to organize the data of a fictitious home budget.

1. List all of the financial commitments. I have done this below. It may seem like a lot, but you can organize this monster list.

1. **Gas**
2. **Electric**
3. **Water and Sewer**
4. **Telephone**
    a. **Land Line**
    b. **Mobile**
5. **Cable/Wireless**
6. **Husband's Paycheck**
7. **Wife's Paycheck**
8. **Mortgage/Rent**
9. **Credit Card**
10. **Home Equity Loan**
11. **Water and Sewer**
12. **Emergency Fund**
13. **Retirement and Investment (IRA, etc.)**
14. **Miscellaneous Expenses**
15. **College Savings**
16. **Wireless**
17. **Cable**
18. **Life Insurance**
19. **Auto Loan**
20. **Student Loan**
21. **Insurance**
22. **Home (if not included in monthly mortgage payment)**
23. **Health**
24. **Long-Term Care**
25. **Auto Insurance**
26. **Utilities:**
27. **Gas**
28. **Investments**
29. **Medical Insurance**
30. **Groceries**
31. **Child Care**
32. **Vacation**
33. **Entertainment (movies, dining out, etc.)**
34. **Clothing**

35. **Gas (automobile)**
36. **Commuting (parking, etc.)**
37. **Charitable Contributions**
38. **Out-of-Pocket Medical Expenses.**

2. Design the structure.
   a. Create the main folder first
   b. Break the items listed into proper categories and create subfolders.
   c. Do this on paper first, and it will eliminate do-overs when you create it on your computer (see page 11).
3. Label the first folder: "Smith Family Budget 2016."
4. Create subfolders of "Smith Family Budget 2016." They are as follows.
   - Income
   - Loans
   - Utilities
   - Insurance Premiums
   - Savings/Investment
   - Miscellaneous Expenses

In figure 5 on the next page is the completed file management structure for "Smith Family Budget 2016." All it takes is for you to decide how you want to design and store your files. Remember—you do not want to scroll through a long list of files. You want quick access to files.

Figure 5

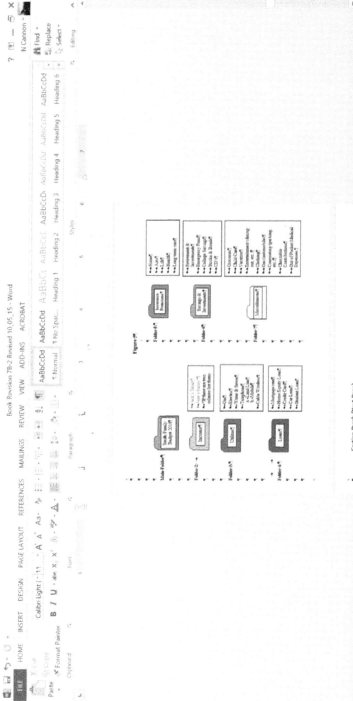

CHAPTER 8
Step-by-Step Instructions

Below, you will find step-by-step instructions to set up "Smith Family Budget 2016."

1. Click on Windows Explorer, located on the task bar at the bottom of the Windows screen. It is in the same row as your start button (Windows 7 and 8.1).

2. Decide where you will store your files. Below is a list of storage mediums you can use to save files on.
   a. desktop
   b. C drive
   c. the cloud
   d. USB drive
   e. CD/DVD

   In this example, we are going to save it to the desktop.

3. Look at the left pane, known as the navigation pane. Click Desktop; this is where you are going to create the first folder.

4. Click on New Folder, on the Menu bar. Now a blank folder appears titled "New Folder."

5. Type "Smith Family Budget 2016" 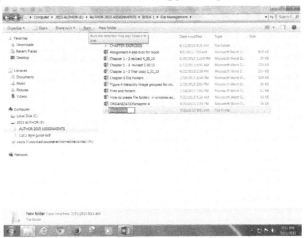 and press Enter.

6. Double-click the new folder you created. This opens this main folder, which is blank, and allows you to create the six new subfolders within it.

7. Click on New Folder on the Menu bar again, and a new blank folder appears again.

8. Type the new file name, "Income," and press Enter.

9. Click the New Folder button and name it "Insurance Premiums."

10. Click the New Folder button and name it "Loans."

11. Click the New Folder button and name it. "Miscellaneous."

12. Click the New Folder button and name it "Savings and Investments."

13. Click the New Folder button and name it "Utilities."

The screen should resemble the figure below.

Name	Date modified	Type	Size
Smith Family Budget 2016	7/21/2015 4:31 PM	File folder	

Click on the folder to open it up, and you should have the following files listed within the main folder.

Name	Date modified	Type	Size
Income	7/21/2015 4:29 PM	File folder	
Insurance Premiums	7/21/2015 4:29 PM	File folder	
Loans	7/21/2015 4:29 PM	File folder	
Miscellaneous	7/21/2015 4:29 PM	File folder	
Savings & Investments	7/21/2015 4:29 PM	File folder	
Utilities	7/21/2015 4:29 PM	File folder	

This is the way it will look in Windows Explorer, once completed:

CHAPTER 9
Another Example: Creating File Management Folders

Remember that in Windows XP, Vista, 7, 8.1, and 10, you use Windows Explorer to store and navigate the contents of your PC.

It is important that you take your time when setting up your file folders, especially when naming them. The name should be simple and easy for you to remember.

If you are a student, you will have one to five classes, maybe even more. How do you manage your files? Well, you could begin with the college name, than the year, then the semester, and finally the subjects. Below is an example. We have a box (representing folders) for each class: English 101, French 101, Math 100, CIS 1000, and Swimming 110. We will now create the structure. Look at figure 6 below.

Figure 6

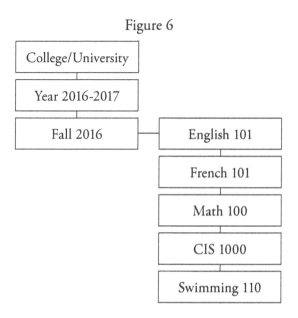

The structure you create could look like the one above. Notice the hierarchy. The top folder is the one with the name of the institution. The subfolder is the year. The next subfolder is the semester, and within the semester folder, you will create five new subject folders. Once you create the folders for each class, you will be able to quickly retrieve the data.

Within these files, you can also create folders for:

1. Assignments for each subject
2. Enrollment records
3. Tuition payments
4. A copy of an unofficial transcript

When the time comes to transfer schools or enter graduate school, you will be able to access all data needed in no time. Make sure you make a backup copy of all the above data on another USB drive, your desktop, an external hard drive, or the cloud.

File folders will make finding your information a breeze. You simply need to take the time and organize them. Have fun!

APPENDIX
Common Questions and Answers

Naming and Creating Folders

1. How do I create a new folder?
   a. Click on the Windows Explorer icon to open it.
   b. Click on the folder you want to save it to. If you want to save it to My Documents, double-click that folder. If you want to save it to the C drive or desktop, double-click one of those folders.
   c. Look in the ribbon and find the group named "New." It will look like the example below.

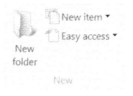

   d. Click on New Folder.
   e. A new folder will appear, and the text will be highlighted in blue.

f. The box is ready to accept the new name—for example, "English." Type the name of the folder, press the Enter key, and the results will be the same as below.

Name

2. What happens when it says New Folder and not the name I tried to give it?

a. Right click the text "New Folder," and a menu will appear. It will look like this.

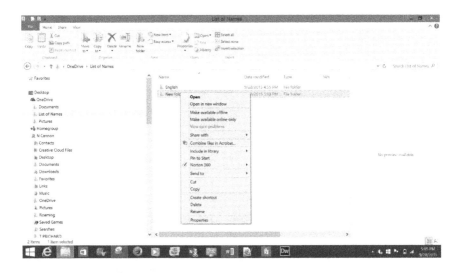

b. Go toward the bottom and left click "Rename."
c. Type the name of the folder.
d. Press the Enter key.
e. If you do not click on the text "New Folder," you will get this menu:

f. If this menu comes up, left click on the white area and it will disappear. Then right click New Folder and type in the name.

3. Can I start the name of my folder with a number or symbol?

You can begin the name of your folder with a number, text, or certain symbols.

4. What symbols cannot be use to name a folder?

You cannot use these symbols, when naming a folder: \ / : * ? " <>

5. Will my folders be listed in alphabetical order?

Yes. When you name the folder and press the Enter key, Windows Explorer will automatically alphabetize it. See the example of Smith Family Budget 2016 on page 20. Notice that the "Smith Family Budget 2016" is the main folder, and the subfolders are listed below and in alpabetical order.

6. Can I place the folders in any order in Windows Explorer?

When you first save a file, they will be placed in alphabetical order once you press the Enter key. Once the files are saved, you can sort your files by Date modified, Name, Type, Size, Date created, Author and more. To do this, go to File Explorer, and on the ribbon, click the View tab, then click on the down arrow of the Sort By icon and a drop down menu will appear.

7. Can I move folders to another area?

You can move a folder to another area. For example, "Smith Family Budget 2016" and its contents can be moved to another area if you want. View the instructions below.

a. Go to Windows Explorer

b. Click the black arrow pointing down on the "Move To" icon (image is below).

c. A submenu will appear. Select a location.

8. What about the layout of the folders in Windows Explorer?

a. In the first column, Windows Explorer lists the file by name. Please note in the above example, you do not see the ".docx" extension, which is used to identify the document as a Word document.

b. In the second column, Windows Explorer lists the date and time the file was last modified.

c. In the third column, Windows Explorer, lists the type of file by name, such as "Microsoft Document."

d. In the fourth column, Windows Explorer lists the size of the folder.

9. How can I find a subfolder if I cannot remember where I placed it?
   a. Within Windows Explorer, on the right side just below the ribbon, is the search box. It is the same search box you use to find your files.
   b. Type the name of the folder within this box.
   c. Remember that everything with a common letter, number, or name will come up, including the subfolder you are looking for.

Creating a New Library

1. Go to the Library group in Windows Explorer.
2. Right click the mouse button.
3. Select New Folder, and a new folder appears.
4. Name the new library.

Naming and Creating Files

10. Can I begin a file name with a symbol or number?
    a. Yes. Here are a few examples.

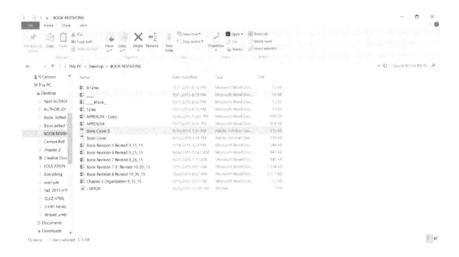

11. Do I need to add ".docx" after the name of my file?
    You do not have to add the ".docx" extension. Word inserts it automatically.
12. What symbol cannot be used to name or save a file?
    a. When you name a file, you cannot use the "*" within the name (e.g., Appendix C*). If you do, you will get the menu and message below stating, "No items match your search." In other words, there are no files with the extension *.

b. You cannot insert the asterisk in the middle of a filename either, or you will get the same menu and message as above. Why? Because the asterisk is a wildcard used by Windows Explorer as a substitute for zero or more characters.

13. How can I find a file or document if I can only remember a portion of the file name?

If you are searching for a file that begins with "for," but you do not remember the rest of the file name, you will type "for*," and all file types that begin with "for" will show up. Here are some possible examples.

   i.   Fortyniners.txt (Text File)

   ii.   Forty thieves.docx (Word)

   iii.   FortyGoldCoins.pptx (PowerPoint)

   iv.   Fortino Sales.xlsx (Excel)

   v.   Formula Racing Payroll.accdb (Access)

14. Can I narrow the search for a file or document without getting all the file types?

a. Yes, you can narrow the search by doing the following.

   i.   You need to remember the type of file it was: Word, Excel, PowerPoint, Access, or another application you may have used.

ii. If the file is a Word document, you can include the document type extension, ".docx," in the name, such as "for*.docx" in the search box, and press Enter.

iii. All files that areWord documents and begin with "for" will come up.

Windows 10 File Management

a. In Windows 10, it is easy to find a subfolder. Simply go to Windows Explorer. The ribbon looks like the image below.

b. Notice that on the ribbon, you do not see a Search tab. To view the Search tab, you will have to click within the search box, and the Search Tools group tab appears in a pinkish color. Now you can click on it.

c. Click on the Search tab and click on "All subfolders" in the location group.

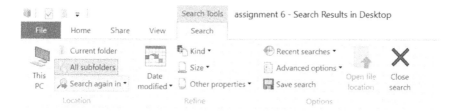

www.ingramcontent.com/pod-product-compliance
Lightning Source LLC
LaVergne TN
LVHW042352060326
832902LV00006B/551